DISCOVER MONTANA TREASURES

Copyright © 2020 by Bryan Schaeffer

All Rights Reserved. No part of this publication may be reproduced,
stored in a retrieval system, or transmitted, in any form or by any means—electronic,
mechanical, photocopying, recording, or otherwise—without prior written permission.

For more information about Bryan or his publication,
please contact the publisher at: discovermontanatreasures.com

Illustrations were created digitally in Adobe Illustrator.

Special thanks to Claudia and Jim Schaeffer.

ISBN: 978-1-7347066-0-4

Printed in the United States of America

HOW TO USE
This Book

THANK YOU FOR PURCHASING Best of the NW's Smart Coloring book *Discover Montana Treasures the Bozone and Beyond*.

Each of the 30 coloring pages has a QR code on the top right corner. This can be scanned by the camera in your mobile phone or device (no app required). See the scenes come to life in full colored animated looping scenes and other bonus videos. Use this as a reference for coloring your page or to make your own unique artwork.

Visit discovermontanatreasures.com for links to GPS maps and more information about each location.

I hope your imagination is activated by these coloring pages so your family can enjoy making memories in these natural places.

Follow on Instagram @bryanschaeffer for new smart coloring pages, videos and artwork. Use #drawntoanimate to share your own colored artwork.

Happy Trails!

NO App Required!

Scan with your phone camera to play colored video clip

ABOUT
The Author

DRAWN TO ANIMATE

RYAN WAS BORN AND RAISED IN Montana and growing up was always curious about what may be lurking around the next switchback, mountain pass or pitch. As an adult he continues to explore Southwest Montana's wild places with his family and friends. He graduated from Pacific Lutheran University in Washington state with a BFA degree in graphic design.

Bryan owns the award-winning creative studio SINTR®, based in Bozeman where he lives with his wife and three daughters. Along with his family and an-eager-to-adventure golden doodle, he enjoys recreating on Montana's public lands. He is the creator of Best of the Northwest, a video and GPS resource for hiking and skiing trails in western Washington which includes over 227 trail videos with affiliated GPS tracks and helpful details about trails.

The author and his sister in the trunk of the family's "SUV" - 1984 Red Rock Lakes National Wildlife Refuge

Discover MONTANA TREASURES
Smart Coloring & Outdoor Activity Book
The Bozone & Beyond

NOT TOO FAR FROM where I grew up is the state's previous capitol, Bannack. Bannack was the site of Montana's first major gold discovery in 1862. During pioneering times, it had been a booming gold town, but now the gold is long gone and all that remains of this once bustling city are some well-preserved structures. Montana's history is filled with many boom and bust cycles like this. However, what persists are the flowing creeks, spring snow melts that give rise to flowers and the never-ending parade of wildlife passing through.

Now it seems the latest gold rush is the land itself. World-class recreation abounds for outdoor enthusiasts and sportsmen alike. Being active in the natural world isn't a luxury in today's hectic lifestyle—it is a necessity if we want to preserve them for future generations. This book will give you some ideas of where a few of these treasures are so you can "discover" them for yourselves.

I hope this activity book inspires your family to get out and make some memories of your own.

Happy Trails!

The New Frontier

Look for the QR code on each page. This can be scanned by your phone to reveal colored page animations. For updates, new illustrations and activities follow on Instagram: @bryanschaeffer

www.discovermontanatreasures.com

State Flower: Bitterroot

State Bird: Western Meadowlark

State Tree: Ponderosa Pine

State Grass: Bluebunch Wheatgrass

State Fish: Cutthroat Trout

State Animal: Grizzly Bear

State Insect: Morning Cloak Butterfly

State Gem: Sapphire

State Dinosaur: Mayasaurus

ALPINE SKI

Big Sky Resort

There once was a girl named Deeds,
who liked to ski through the trees.
One day on the slopes,
she found the coldsmoke
and sailed through the plumes like the breeze.

NO App Required!
BEST OF THE NW
Scan with your phone camera to play colored video clip

Skiing Big Sky Resort
Big Sky Ski Area, Gallatin National Forest

HIKE/CLIMB

Palisade Falls

In winter, an ice-covered column to climb,
In summer, a waterfall sublime.
Summer's misty spray
Becomes winter play
And the cascades are frozen in time.

Distance: 1.2 miles round trip
Elevation Gain: 250 feet
Visit: discovermontanatreasures.com for maps & more.

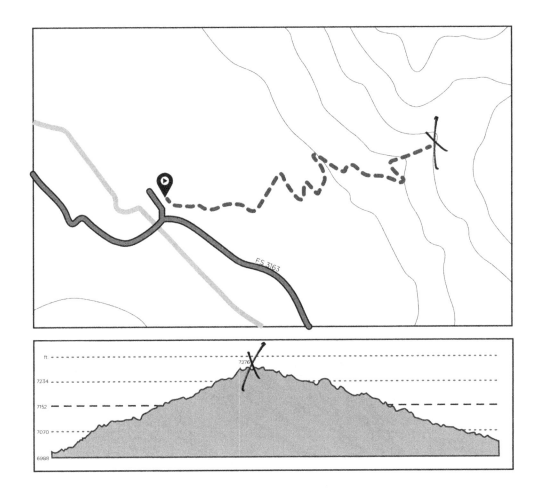

Hiking Palisade Falls
Hyalite's 80' cascade over columnar basalt

HIKE

Beehive Basin

We hike upward on a trail lush
With meadows of lupine and paintbrush.
Carved by a glacier,
Worth the climb, for sure,
We marvel at the vistas—no need to rush!

Distance: 7 miles round trip
Elevation Gain: 1,500 feet
Visit: discovermontanatreasures.com for maps & more.

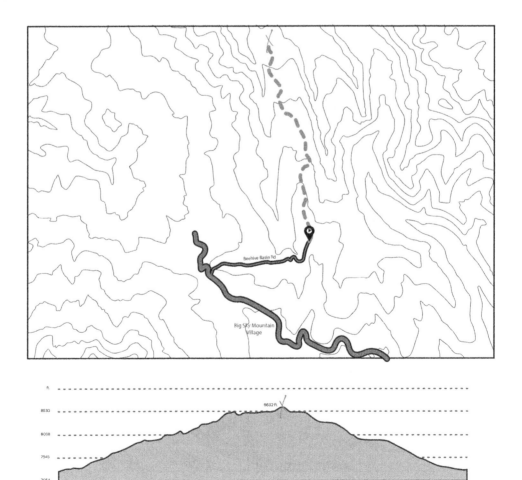

Hiking Beehive Basin
Majestic glacial cirque at the foot of the Spanish Peaks

HIKE

Grotto Falls

Every season is nice;
This one has ice.
The gurgling creek
In mid-winter's sleep
Will lure you more than twice.

Distance: 2.5 miles round trip from Hayalite Lake Parking lot
Elevation Gain: 580 feet
Visit: discovermontanatreasures.com for maps & more.

Hiking Grotto Falls
Hyalite's popular summer hike with a different look for winter

CLIMB

Crocodile Rock

NO App Required!
BEST OF THE NW
Scan with your phone camera to play colored video clip

Atop the ridge like a flag,
Protecting this rock climbing crag,
A reptile you'll spot
From the parking lot.
Who sees it first has rights to brag!

Climb Crocodile Rock
Hyalite's craggy guard animal

FLOAT

Hyalite Reservoir

Locals find it hard to ignore
The draw of Hyalite Reservoir:
Camping, boating, hiking,
Mountain or road biking—
The options are there to explore.

NO App Required!

BEST OF THE NW

Scan with your phone camera to play colored video clip

Float Hyalite Lake

Canoe, kayak, drift, innertube, stand up paddleboard—the choice is yours

SKI

Beehive Basin

Beehive is a winter canvas
Whose painters' marks soon vanish.
The tracks we make
Don't seem to take
With the snow's ever-changing status.

Distance: 7 miles round trip
Elevation Gain: 1,500 feet
Visit: discovermontanatreasures.com for maps & more.

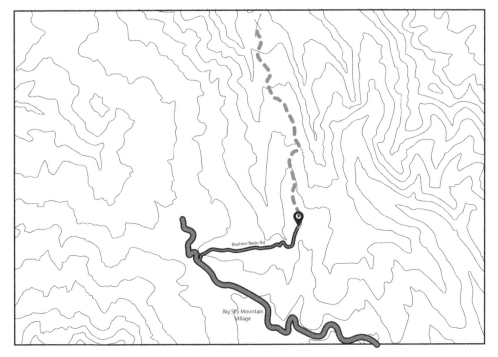

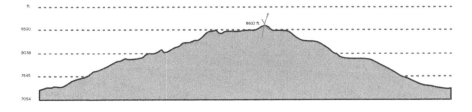

Skinning Up Beehive Basin
Majestic glacial cirque at the foot of the Spanish Peaks

MOUNTAIN BIKE

The Wall of Death

When you ride the Wall of Death trail
You don't want your steering to fail.
Keep rubber side down,
Both tires on the ground,
Then coast into town for an ale.

Distance: 7 miles round trip
Elevation Gain: 1,500 feet
Visit: discovermontanatreasures.com for maps & more.

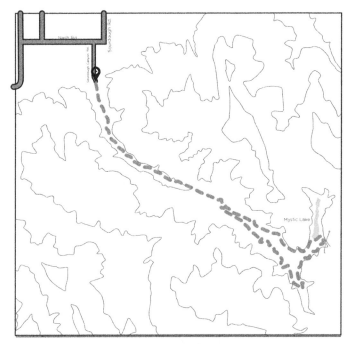

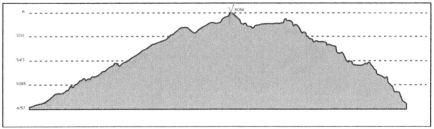

Mountain Biking the Wall of Death Trail
The Wall of Death trail is an aptly named trail, but there are biking trails on the Gallatin National Forest for all ability levels.

SKI

Hyalite Tour

Looping the lake, you fly through the trees
With a kick and a glide, you ski with ease.
Lake views, mountain views,
Keep skiing, don't snooze—
Many trail choices to ski where you please!

Cross Country Ski
Loop Hyalite Lake, with plenty of trails to lose yourself on

ROCK CLIMB

Gallatin Canyon

Rock Climb Spare Rib
A classic old-school trad two pitch "5.8" above the Gallatin River

NO App Required!
Scan with your phone camera to play colored video clip

Route setters, they fib
When rating "Spare Rib."
The climb is great,
But to call it "5.8"—
Why are old-school climbers so glib?

BIKE

Bozeman

Bozemanites love the "M" trail for hiking
So consider getting there by biking.
Take the GVLT trail
To avoid the parking lot travail,
And hop off the bike to go walking!

Distance: 80 Miles GVLT Trails Mainstreet to Mountains
Elevation Gain: Minimal
Visit: discovermontanatreasures.com for maps & more.

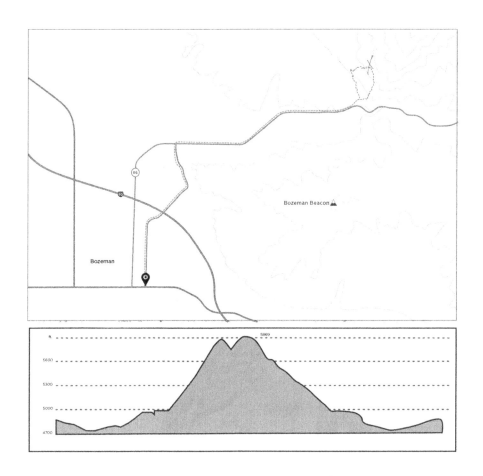

Biking Bozeman
Bike GVLT trails, Mainstreet to the Mountains

HIKE/RUN

The Triple Tree Trail

Distance: 4.5 miles round trip
Elevation Gain: 800 feet
Visit: discovermontanatreasures.com for maps & more.

A Bozeman trail that's easy to find.
So don't leave your dog behind.
A leash is polite
And keeps him in sight
As the trail winds.

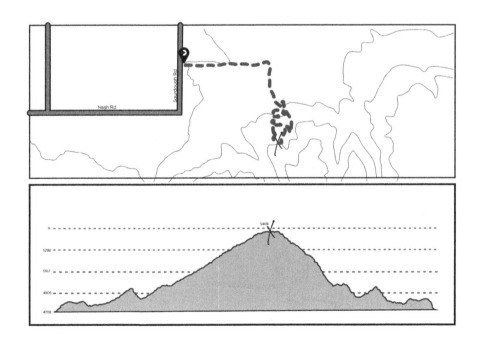

Hiking Triple Tree Trail
Mind your manners on Bozeman's popular trails to make the experience enjoyable for all.

HIKE

Pine Creek Falls Trail

Distance: 3 miles round trip
Elevation Gain: 300 feet
Visit: discovermontanatreasures.com for maps & more.

A pleasant stroll along Pine Creek—
Fairy houses and treasures we seek.
A slight sloping ridge
To cross Pine Creek bridge
To soak in Pine Creek Falls mystique.

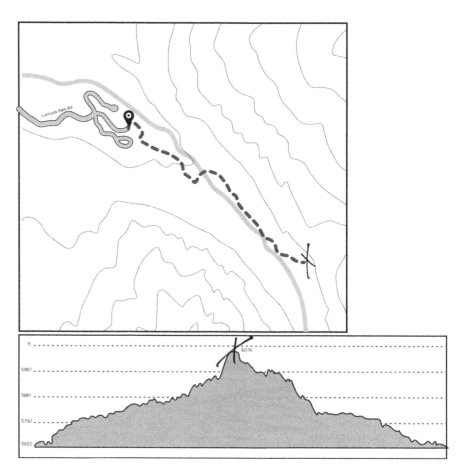

Hiking Pine Creek Trail
Easy does it—crossing the Pine Creek bridge with a little emotional support from Fluffy Bunny

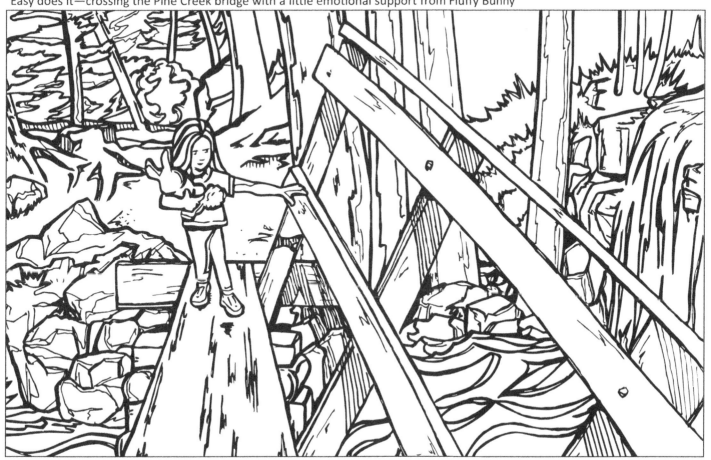

SKI

Fawn Pass

This majestic animal of the West
Represents Yellowstone at its best.
Accepting their plight,
For survival they fight,
And with grit they endure winter's test.

Distance: 8 miles round trip
Elevation Gain: 1,500 feet
Visit: discovermontanatreasures.com for maps & more.

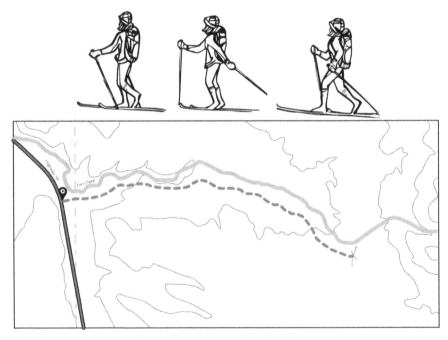

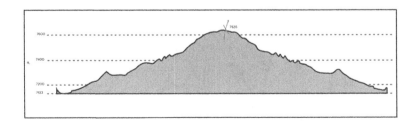

NO App Required!
Scan with your phone camera to play colored video clip

Ski Fawn Pass
Explore Yellowstone National Park in the solitude of winter.

ROAD TRIP

The Pioneers

A place that never seems to change.
Mountains to explore,
Meadows and more,
Outdoor adventures I would not exchange.

Y CHILDHOOD STOMPING grounds. These mountains haven't changed much since I was a kid. Explore the Dillon area and the Beaverhead Valley: Torrey Peak, Pioneer Mountains, Beaverhead-Deerlodge National Forest , Crystal Park where you can dig for quartz crystals, Lemhi Pass where Lewis and Clark stood, Grasshopper Valley-Maverick Mountain Ski Area, Bannack State Park and the Humbug Spires Wilderness study area North of Dillon.

Torrey Mountain
In the heart of the Pioneers.

CLIMB

Sacajawea and Hardscrabble Peaks

We rise before dawn to summit this peak,
Aiming for the early season solitude we seek.
At the top, a surprise—
This kid goat arrives
And we share a view that can't be beat.

Distance: 9.6 miles round trip
Elevation Gain: 1,500 feet
Visit: discovermontanatreasures.com for maps & more.

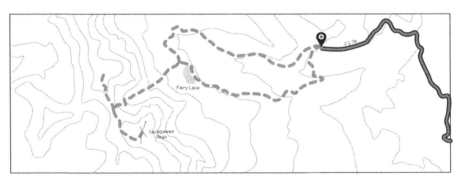

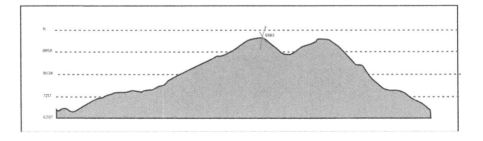

Climb Sacajawea Peak
The Bridgers' locals also enjoy peak experiences first thing in the morning.

CHILL

Flathead Lake

Montana's largest body of water
Is most pleasant when the weather's hotter.
So for goodness sake
Take a dip in the lake!
But keep your eyes peeled for the monster.

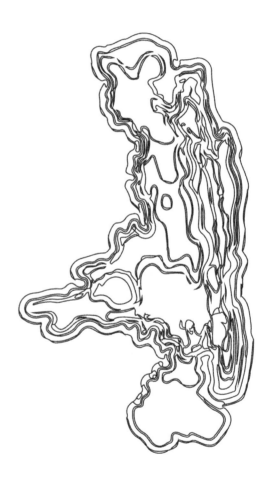

Flathead Lake
Hanging out at the family reunion; Hammock City—Flathead Lutheran Bible Camp, Lakeside, Montana.

GLACIER NATIONAL PARK
The Highline Trail

A place for your consideration
When planning your summer vacation,
With miles of trails,
Where nature prevails,
Glacier is a hiking destination.

Distance: 11.8 miles round trip
Elevation Gain: 1,950 feet
Visit: discovermontanatreasures.com for maps & more.

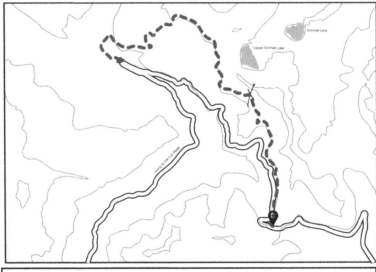

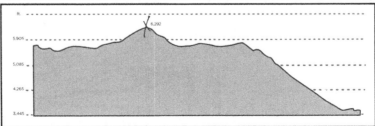

The Highline Trail
The Highline Trail skirts the Garden Wall above the Going-to-the-Sun Road in Glacier National Park.

Twenty year high beargrass bloom—backpacking along the Garden Wall, Glacier National Park

GLACIER NATIONAL PARK

Gunsight Pass

In Glacier we need to take care
To watch for the presence of bear.
But when, with surprise,
One appears before your eyes,
The encounter can be quite a scare.

Distance: 20 miles round trip
Elevation Gain: 3,727 feet east to west
Visit: discovermontanatreasures.com for maps & more.

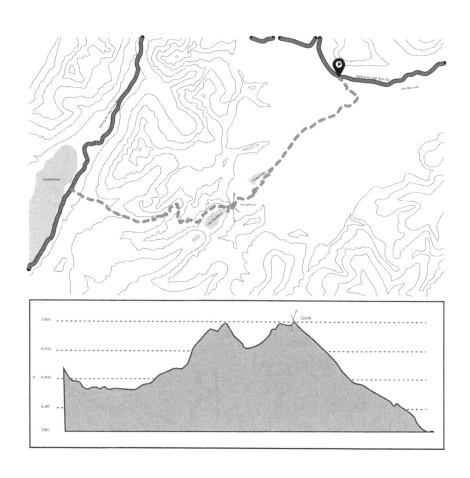

Hiking Gunsight Pass
Hikers aren't the only critters using the trails.

BACKPACK

Spanish Peaks

Backpacking in the Spanish Peaks—
Would be nice to be there for weeks!
So much to explore,
From peaks to lakeshore
With climbs that will build your physique.

Distance: 24 miles round trip
Elevation Gain: 4,767
Visit: discovermontanatreasures.com for maps & more.

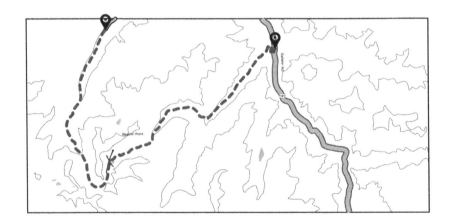

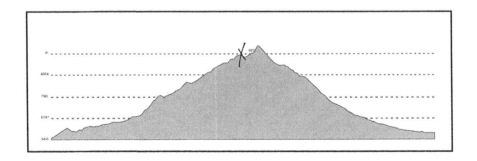

The Spanish Peaks
Backpacking the Spanish Peaks

CLIMB

Granite Peak

Trails, talus, and rock you must navigate
To reach the top of the state.
Miles and miles you'll go
On Froze to Death Plateau,
Then up the ridge, if weather cooperates.

Distance: 30 miles round trip
Elevation Gain: 9,960
Visit: discovermontanatreasures.com for maps & more.

Bonus Video!
BEST OF THE NW
Scan with your phone camera to play colored video clip

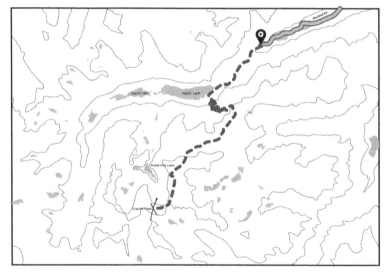

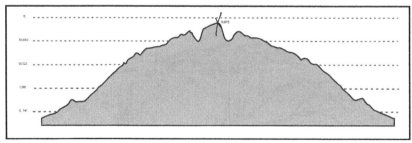

Granite Peak
The top of Montana: Granite Peak—Beartooth Mountains, Custer/Gallatin National Forest

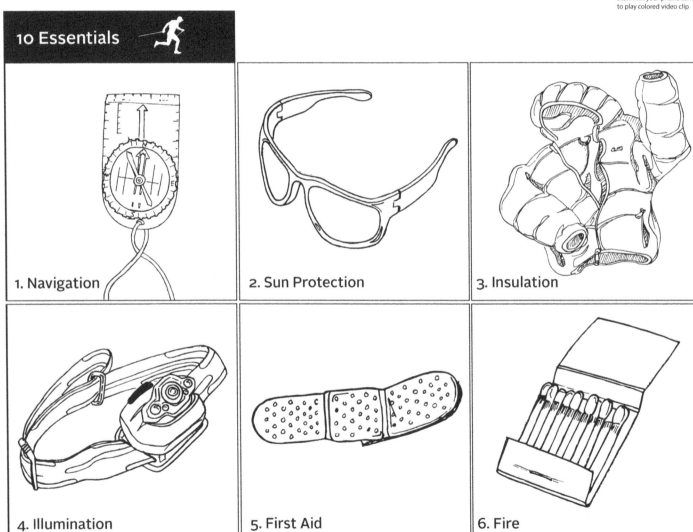

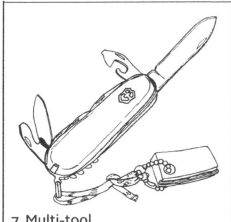
7. Multi-tool

8. Nutrition

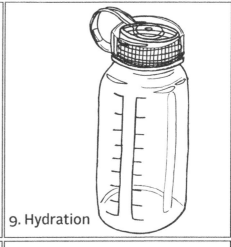
9. Hydration

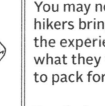
10. Emergency Shelter

You may notice that veteran hikers bring less gear, having the experience to anticipate what they will and won't need to pack for each outing.

Familarize yourself with your equipment and gear systems.

©2019 @bryanschaeffer

10 ESSENTIALS — BEST OF THE NW

CANOE

The Missouri River Breaks

To canoe on the Missouri
Is to paddle into history.
Where wolves and grizzlies roamed,
Lewis and Clark explored,
And settlers entered this land of mystery.

Canoeing on the Missouri River

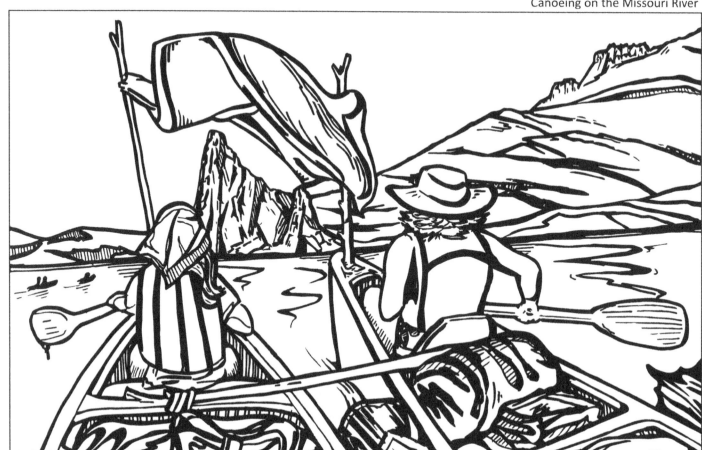

SNOWBOARD

Bridger Bowl

Strap your boots to a board
As many times as you can afford,
To shred down a line
Feeling so fine—
Such joy is its own reward!

Snowboard Bridger Bowl

The Bridger cloud drops copious amounts of cold smoke for the enjoyment of ridge riders.

HIKE/RUN THE RIDGE

The Bridgers

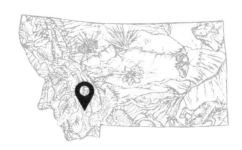

I first climbed Bridger Peak in the dark,
For then I was only a spark—
Safe in the tummy
Of my athletic mummy,
As she carried me to the mark.

Distance: 20 miles
Elevation Gain: 6,800 feet 9,500 foot loss
Visit: discovermontanatreasures.com for maps & more.

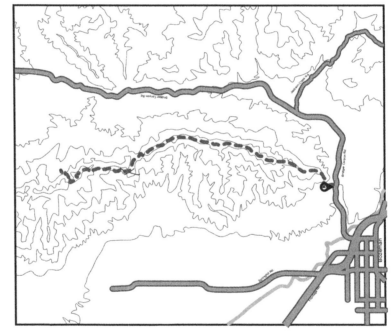

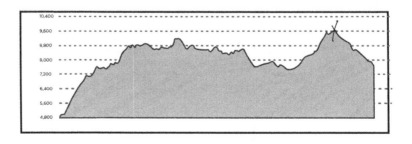

The Bridger Ridge
Bozeman's big back (or front) yard

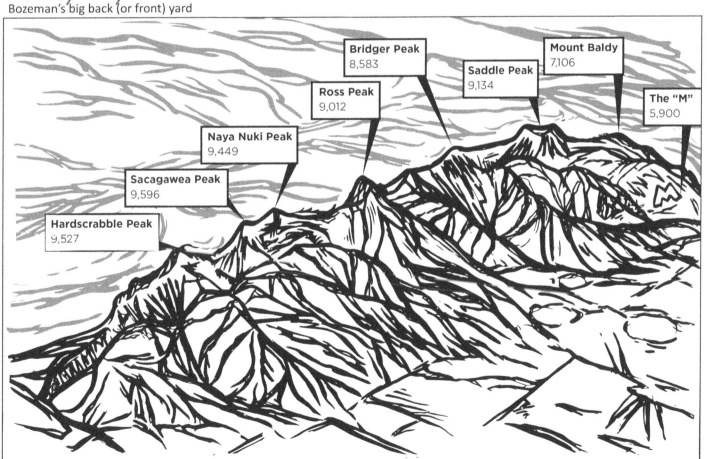

BACKPACK

Hilgard Basin

Hike the high country of Hilgard Basin
To gain peace of mind and appreciation
Of a skyline of peaks
And the solitude one seeks—
An alpine paradise for the soul's regeneration!

Distance: 20 miles
Elevation Gain: 3,650 feet
Visit: discovermontanatreasures.com for maps & more.

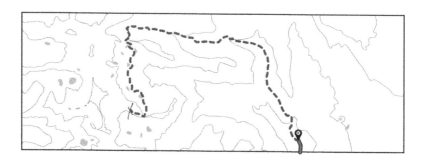

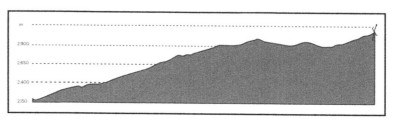

NO App Required!

BEST OF THE NW

Scan with your phone camera to play colored video clip

Hike Hilgard Basin
Hiking and camping, plenty of fishing and exploring to be had in Hilgard Basin, Lee Metcalf Wilderness, Gallatin National Forest

WILDLIFE

Bozeman

Montana is full of wild game,
Without them, it wouldn't be the same—
To hunt and to fish,
We wouldn't get our wish
If all the animals were tame.

NO App Required!

Scan with your phone camera to play colored video clip

Basking in the golden light,
A creature of power and might.
A meal he did need,
A deer carcass to feed.
He ate his fill, then took flight.

SOAK

The Boiling River

You might catch a shiver
Hiking to the Boiling River.
The freezing water
Gets much hotter
When Yellowstone's thermals deliver.

Distance: 1.3 miles
Elevation Gain: 50 feet
Visit: discovermontanatreasures.com for maps & more.

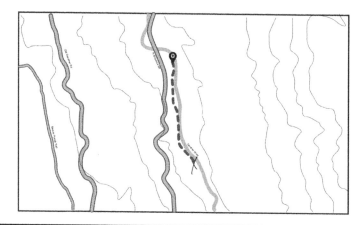

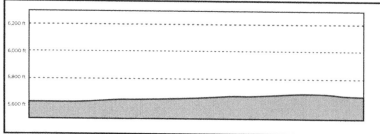

NO App Required!

Scan with your phone camera to play colored video clip

The Boiling River
Gardner River, Yellowstone National Park

FISH

Montana

As the summer sun begins to set,
With a splash, the lure is wet.
The fishing day went fast—
Just one more "last cast"
And I'll land one this time, I bet!

Fishing Flathead Lake

Second to last cast. Thanks to restoration efforts the state's largest lake is getting bluer and the fish are taking notice!

BIRD WATCHING

Western Meadowlark

Identify the distinctive mark
On the chest of the Meadowlark.
You may have heard
The song of Montana's state bird,
Emanating from where the yellow goes dark.

Montana Treasure
Western Meadowlark framing the Spanish Peaks, Gallatin National Forest

From outside to inside the colors of the rainbow can be remembered by the abbreviation ROY-G-BIV:

Wildlife Watching
Hayden Valley—Yellowstone National Park

The rainbow is nature's promise
Of renewal and peace and bliss.
We revel in the light,
The colors give sight
To the spectrum of life we don't want to miss.

I hope this book activates your imagination and feeds your appetite for adventure.

Follow on Instagram @bryanschaeffer to discover new treasures, new free coloring page downloads, outdoor recreation tips and more.

Happy Trails!

Made in the USA
Monee, IL
27 March 2020